Flip for Non-Fiction Comprehension

by Emily Cayuso

Maupin House *by*
capstone
professional

Flip for Non-Fiction Comprehension
by Emily Cayuso

Layout/Design by Mickey Cuthbertson
Illustrations by Josh Clark

Library of Congress Cataloging-in-Publication Data

Cayuso, Emily, 1954-
 Flip for non-fiction comprehension / by Emily Cayuso.
     p. cm.
 Includes bibliographical references and index.
 ISBN-13: 978-1-934338-37-7 (pbk.)
 ISBN-10: 1-934338-37-0 (pbk.)
 1. Reading comprehension. 2. Reading (Elementary)--Activity programs.
 3. Reading (Middle school)--Activity programs. I. Title.
 LB1573.7.C39 2009
 372.47--dc22
                         2008046732

Also by Emily Cayuso:
 Flip for Comprehension
 Flip for Word Work
 Dar la Vuelta a la Comprensión
 Designing Teacher Study Groups

ISBN-13: 978-1-934338-37-7

Maupin House Publishing, Inc. by Capstone Professional.
1710 Roe Crest Drive
North Mankato, MN 56003
888-262-6135
www.maupinhouse.com

Publishing Professional Resources that Improve Classroom Performance

Printed in China.
052014 008267

Table of Contents

Table of Contents (cont'd.)

Introduction

Because the majority of reading done in life is non-fiction, the ability of students to read and understand non-fiction texts is a necessary skill that must be explicitly taught (Harvey, 1998). Teachers must expose students to many varied experiences with non-fiction texts in order to prepare them to read and write effectively, both for information and to achieve literacy success. In addition, educators must teach the specific strategies, text features, and text structures that are necessary for students to access and understand non-fiction texts. The use of these texts builds upon a child's natural inherent curiosity of the world, and the more exposure and opportunities to interact with informational texts the better equipped our students will be to be life-long readers and writers.

This packet is designed to provide teachers with ready-to-use comprehension ideas that can be implemented before, during, or after the reading of non-fiction texts. Many of the ideas can be used in various classroom settings.

Small Reading Groups: The teacher can use these activities with small reading groups as an extension to questioning and comprehension work with non-fiction texts.

Literacy Centers: This packet can be a stand-alone comprehension center or added to an existing center such as the writing, listening, or independent reading/library center. The activities can enhance and extend the work students are assigned to do in the center.

Literature Circles: Ideas presented in this packet can be used as a guide to facilitate discussion and/or structure written responses or projects for the group to work on and share.

Read Alouds: The teacher can use many of the ideas to facilitate, enhance, and extend student understanding of the text read aloud.

Independent Writing: Many of the activities can be used as a springboard for student writing and reader response to the texts read.

Introduction (cont'd.)

Independent Reading: Many of the activities can be used to facilitate the "sharing time" that follows independent reading. In addition, if the teacher holds one-on-one conferences during the reading time, these activities can provide the teacher with a means of checking student understanding of the independently read text.

Content-Area Reading and Writing: The activities can be used as an additional follow-up and comprehension check to content-area reading and units of study such as in science and social studies.

To ensure student success with *Flip for Non-fiction Comprehension*, it is important to model the strategy with the students first, followed by enough teacher-guided practice before the student is expected to apply the strategy and/or activity independently.

These strategies/activities can be done either as oral or written exercises. They can be used to guide group discussions or activities completed independently in student reading journals, on chart paper, or on construction paper. Likewise, the activities can be done in student pairs or small cooperative groups.

The ideas in this packet are listed alphabetically by title of the activity. You may use the Table of Contents as a quick reference guide or simply scan through the activities. Look at the idea, the type of text your students are currently reading, and the particular comprehension needs you want to address. Perhaps your teacher's guide suggests an idea similar to one you find here. You may also find that certain stories naturally lend themselves to a particular activity. However you make your selections, remember that developing a repertoire of good comprehension strategies for all readers is the goal.

How to Use This Book

- Use this book with a small group, whole class, or as part of an independent center.

- Stand the book up like a tent to the page you want your students to work on.

- Insert any other information needed directly onto the page using sticky notes or cover-up tape. You may also clip a clear transparency sheet over the page and write on it.

- Model with your students how to successfully complete the activity.

- Provide the necessary materials to complete the activity.

Attribute Comparison

- **Make a comparison chart like this.**

- **Think about the attributes of two persons, animals, objects, or groups discussed in the text.**

- **Fill in the chart.**

- **You may add more attributes if you like.**

Attributes	X:_____	Y:_____
1.		
2.		
3.		

Bolded Words

- **Find all the bolded words in the text and write them on a sheet of paper.**

- **Use each word in a sentence of your own.**

- **Draw a picture to go with each sentence.**

- **Use your text and the glossary for help.**

Tropical **rainforests** are home to the largest and the smallest, the loudest and the quietest of all land **animals**, as well as some of the most endearing and most beautiful, most dangerous, strangest looking animals on **earth**. You've probably heard of some of them: **tree frogs**, **toucans**, **parrots**, **gorillas**, and **tarantulas** all make their home in tropical rainforests.

RAINFOREST

Brochures

- **Make a brochure about** _____.
- **Use your text to help.**

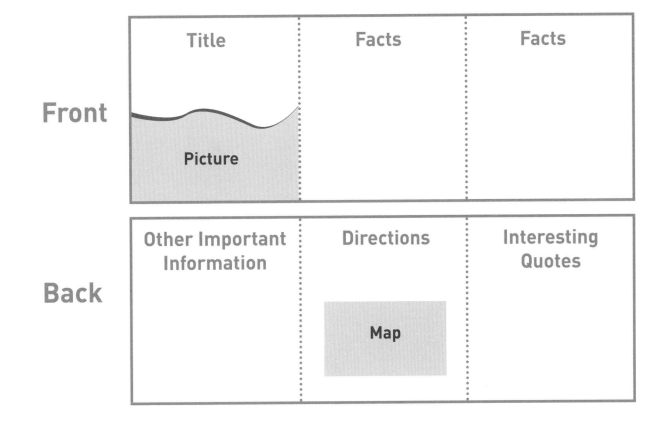

Front

| Title | Facts | Facts |
| Picture | | |

Back

| Other Important Information | Directions | Interesting Quotes |
| | Map | |

Cause and Effect

- **Make a chart like the one below.**

- **Find all cause and effect relationships that happened in the text and put them in the chart.**

Cause	Effect

Close-Up

- Draw a close-up of _____ that was discussed in the text.

- Label all the parts of your drawing.

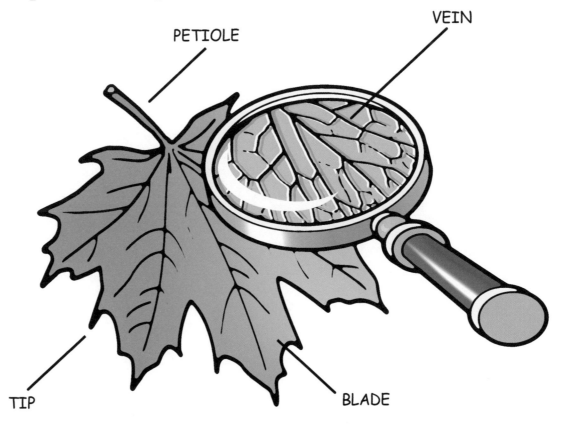

PETIOLE

VEIN

TIP

BLADE

Coding the Text

- **Make a chart like the one below.**

- **As you read the text, write down ideas and information that fits into each category on the chart.**

★ = Interesting	BK = Background Knowledge	? = Questions
C = Confusing	I = Important	L = Learned Something New

Concentration

- **Write each bolded word from the text on an index card.**

- **On a separate index card write the definition of each bolded word.**

- **Place the cards upside down.**

- **Take turns with your partner(s) matching the bolded word with the correct definition.**

- **Keep score if you like. The one who makes the most matches is the winner.**

Concept Map

- Make a concept map like the one below.

- Fill in the map about _____ that was discussed in the text.

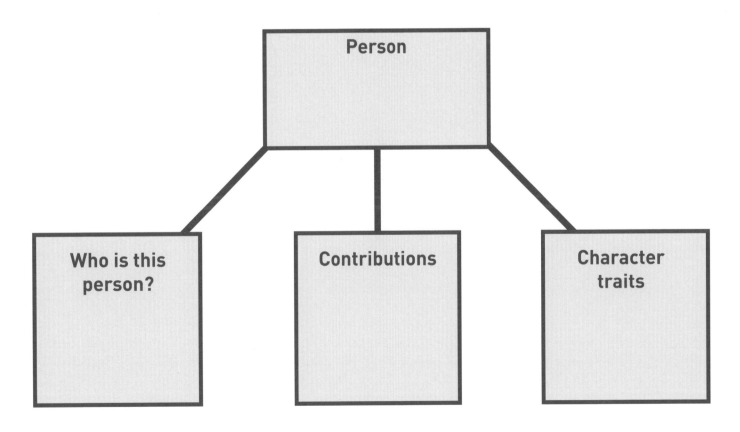

Convention Hunt

- **Make a chart like this one.**

- **Go on a "convention hunt" with non-fiction texts in your classroom.**

- **Write the title of the text under each section if it has an example of the convention listed.**

Labels	Captions	Photographs	Comparisons
Cut-Aways	Bolded Words	Headings	Close-ups
Table of Contents	Index	Glossary	Maps

Convention Purposes

- **Make a chart like the one below.**

- **As you read the text, identify and record in the first column any conventions related to the appearance of the text, for example, labels, photographs, captions, headings, and bold print.**

- **In the second column, explain the purpose of the convention.**

Conventions	Purposes

Cutaway

- **Make a cutaway drawing of the _____ that was discussed in the text.**

- **Label all the parts of your drawing.**

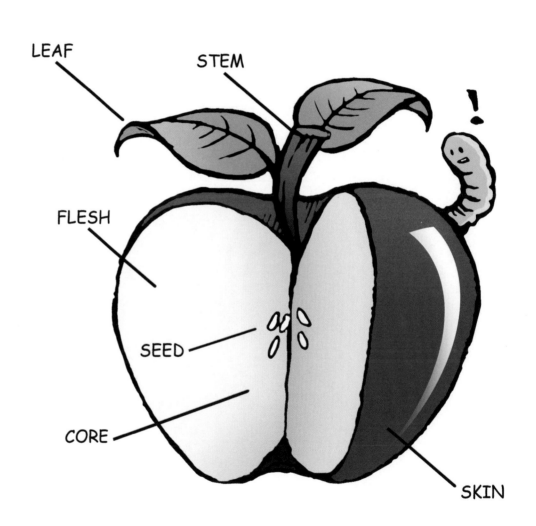

LEAF

STEM

FLESH

SEED

CORE

SKIN

Cycles

- **Write down the major cycles discussed in the text that happen to _____ on index cards.**

- **Exchange the cards with your partner and see if he/she can arrange the cards in the correct order.**

- **Check yourself with the text.**

- **Take a sheet of paper and glue the cards in the correct order on it.**

- **Draw a picture to match each cycle.**

The larva hatches from the egg.

A beautiful, flying adult emerges.

It turns into a pupa.

A butterfly starts its life as an egg.

Dear Diary

- **Write a diary entry.**
- **Record** _____ **historical event from the point of view of** _____.
- **Use your text to help.**

Dear Diary,

What an exciting day! I went out with my kite during a storm. First I noticed the strands of the kite string stood out every way. Then, all of a _sudden, I felt an electrical_ spark as my hand held the key I had tied to the end of the kite string. I think I discovered electricity. Wow!

Benjamin Franklin
June 1752

Describe It

- **Make a chart like the one below.**

- **Write descriptive words about _____ that was discussed in the text.**

- **Use your text, a dictionary, or a thesaurus to add as many words as you can to the chart.**

Adjectives	Adverbs

Determining Importance: Top Ten

- **After reading the text, determine the ten most important points to remember.**

- **Create a "top ten" list of important points.**

- **Number 1 will be the most important point, with the other points decreasing in importance up to number 10.**

Top Ten about _____

1.
2.
3.
4.
5.
6.
7.
8.
9.
10.

Direct Quotes

- **Locate direct quotes said by** _____ **in the text.**

- **On the front of index cards write the *direct quote(s).***

- **On the back of the index cards write your *personal response* to the quote(s).**

Direct Quote

"Our lives begin to end the day we become silent about things that matter"

Martin Luther King Jr.

Personal Response

I think we must always speak up for what we believe in and care about what is happening in the world.

Bobby

Draw and Label I

- Draw a picture or diagram of the _____ that was discussed in the text.

- Label its parts with the correct vocabulary word.

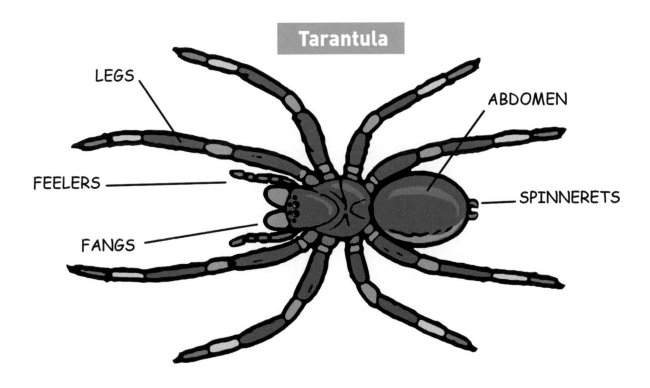

Tarantula

LEGS

ABDOMEN

FEELERS

SPINNERETS

FANGS

Draw and Label II

- **Draw a picture or diagram of the _____ that was discussed in the text.**

- **Your partner should then label its parts with the correct vocabulary words.**

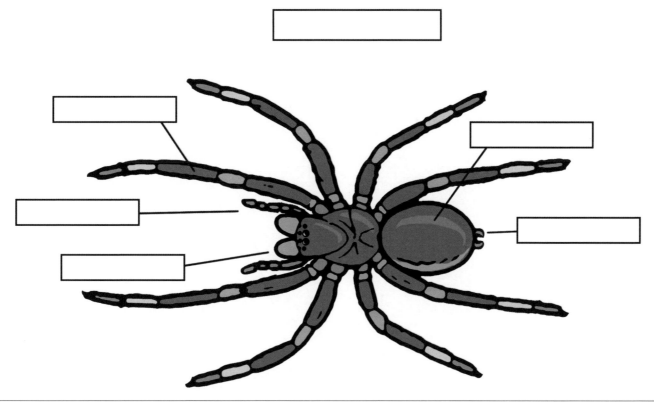

Facts About...

- **Make a chart like the one below.**

- **Fill out the chart with as many facts as you can about _____ that was discussed in the text.**

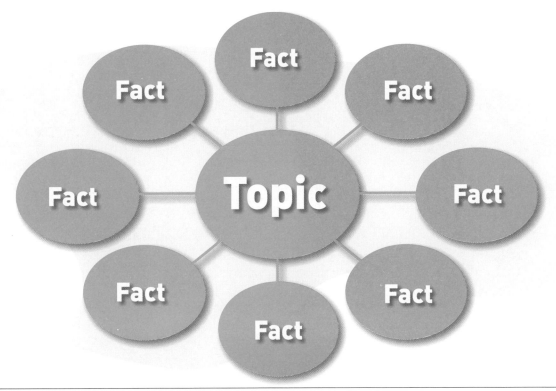

Facts and Opinions

- **Make a chart like the one below.**

- **Write facts and opinions from the text in each column.**

- **Add other facts and opinions not in the text to each column.**

- **On the back of your chart, explain in your own words what makes each a fact or opinion.**

Facts	Opinions

Famous Quotes

● **Fill out the chart below about the historical figure you are studying right now.**

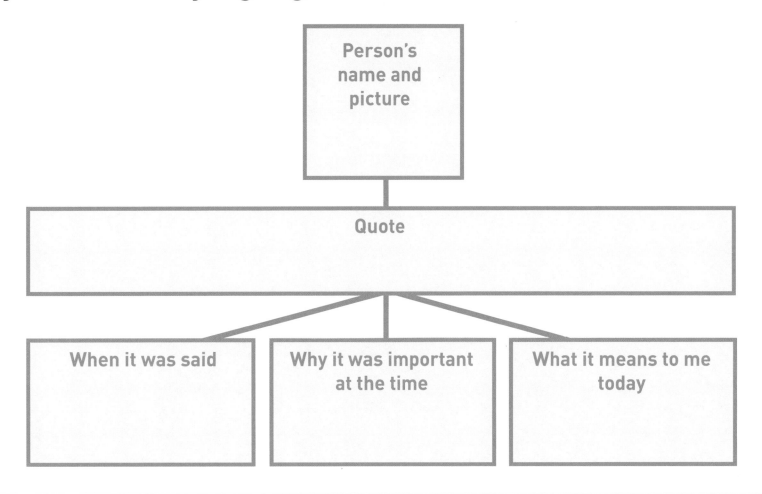

Person's name and picture

Quote

When it was said

Why it was important at the time

What it means to me today

Field Trip Observations

- **Make a chart like the one below.**

- **Reflect on the field trip the class took to_____ by filling in the chart.**

Surprising Observations	Important Things to Remember
Best and Worst about the Trip	**What I Want to Do More Research on**

Glossary Word Sort

- **Write each glossary word from the text on an index card.**

- **Sort the words by whatever method you like.**

- **Make a chart to illustrate your system. Label the categories.**

- **Add other words that fit in each category you created. Use your text for help.**

Glossary Word Sort

Guinness Book of World Records

- **What is a world record or feat you would like to find out about?**

- **Use *Guinness World Records* to find your answer.**

- **Fill out the chart below.**

- **On the back of the chart draw a picture of the record-breaking feat.**

Questions I Have:		
Who:	What:	When:
Where:	Why:	How:

Headings

- **Divide your paper into boxes. There should be one box for each heading found in the text.**

- **Write each heading in a box.**

- **Under each heading write the main idea of the section.**

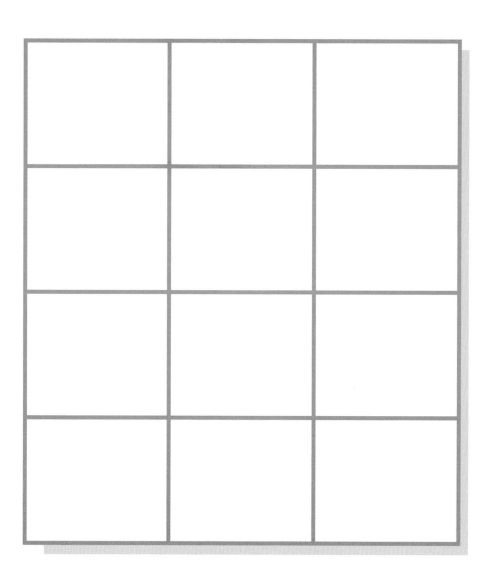

Hear Ye, Hear Ye

● **Make a chart like the one below.**

● **Using the _____ speech discussed in the text, fill out the chart.**

Title of Speech:		
Who Gave Speech:	Intended Audience:	Important Points:
Main Idea of Speech:		

Historical Event Key Information

● **Draw and fill in the graphic with the key information about _____ historical event from the text.**

Who:	When:	Where:

What Happened:	Why It Was Important:

Historical Fiction

- **Make a chart like the one below.**

- **Find examples in the text of fiction and non-fiction and fill in the chart.**

- **Use the column titled "Reason" to explain why you placed the examples where you did.**

Fiction Examples	Reason	Non-Fiction Examples	Reason

How-To

- **List all the steps in the correct order related to _____ from the text.**

- **Use as many steps as you need.**

1

2

3

4

Index Search

● **Make a chart like the one below.**

● **Write questions you want answered from the text based on a picture walk of the title, headings, and conventions.**

● **Using only the index of the text, write the page number you feel will have the answer to your questions.**

● **Check the page number to see if your answer is there. Write the answer and verify that the index matched the answer.**

Title:			
Questions	Index Page Number	Answers	Did the Answer Match the Index?
1)	1)	1)	1)
2)	2)	2)	2)
3)	3)	3)	3)
4)	4)	4)	4)
5)	5)	5)	5)

Informal Outline

- **Use bullets and indentations to outline the text.**

- **Put key information next to each bullet and details about the key information next to each indentation.**

Outline on:_____
- **Key Information**
  - Details
  - Details
  - Details
- **Key Information**
  - Details
  - Details
  - Details
- **Key Information**
  - Details
  - Details
  - Details

KWL Charts I

● **Draw and complete the KWL chart your teacher put a check mark next to using the text you are reading.**

☐

What I Know	What I Wonder	What I Learned

☐

What I Know	What I Wonder	What I Learned	What I Still Wonder

☐

What I Learned	Where in the Text I Found It

KWL Charts II

● **Draw and complete the KWL chart your teacher put a check mark next to using the text you are reading.**

☐

What I Know	What I Wonder	What I Learned	How It Affected Me

☐

What I Know	What I Learned	What I Still Wonder

☐

Wonderings	Answers I Discovered

KWL Charts III

● **Draw and complete the KWL chart your teacher put a check mark next to using the text you are reading.**

☐

What I Know	What I Learned	Proof

☐

What I Know	What I Wonder

☐

What I Know	What I Learned

Letter To...

- **Write a letter to _____,** whom you have been reading about in the text.

- **What would you like to ask him/her?**

- **What do you want to tell him/her?**

The Main Idea

○ **Draw and fill in the graphic with the main idea and supporting details from the text.**

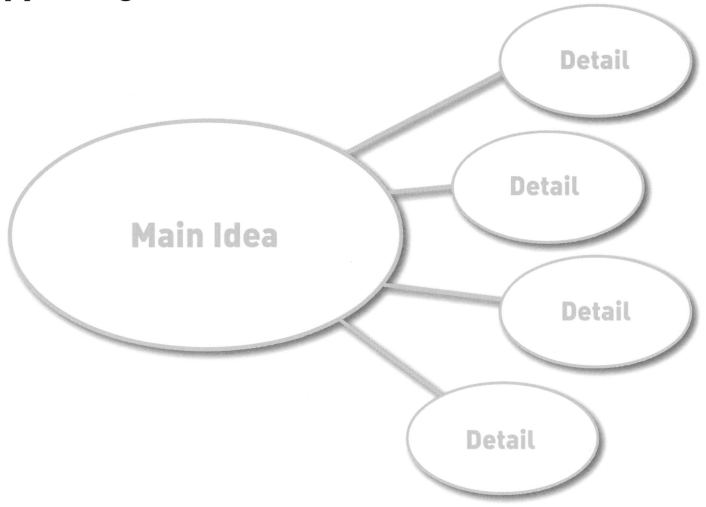

Making Connections

- **Make a chart like the one to the right.**

- **Think about the text you read.**

- **Can you make a *text-to-self*, *text-to-text*, or *text-to-world* connection?**

- **Write the connections you made in the chart.**

Text to Self	Text to Text	Text to Word

Map It Out

- **Draw a map showing _____ that was discussed in the text.**

- **Label all the important information on the map.**

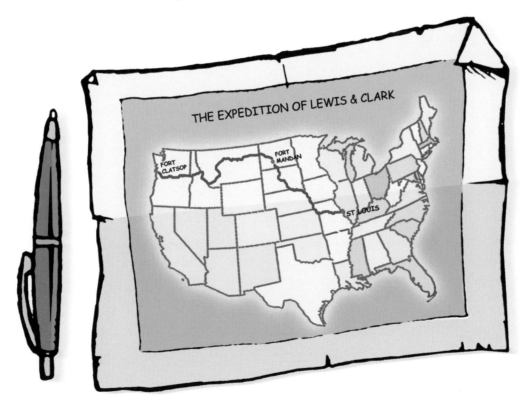

THE EXPEDITION OF LEWIS & CLARK

FORT CLATSOP

FORT MANDAN

ST LOUIS

Mind Picture

- **What picture is in your mind after reading the text about _____?**

- **On a sheet of paper write the title of the event.**

- **Draw and color the mind picture you have of the event after reading about it.**

TITLE: THE WRIGHT BROTHERS' FIRST FLIGHT

Newspaper Discussion

● **Make a chart like the one below.**

● **Take the newspaper and find the**
_____ section of the paper.

● **Pick an article from that section.**

● **Fill out the chart based on the contents of the article chosen.**

Title:		
Who:	What:	When:
Where:	Why:	How:
Main Idea:		

Note-Taking

- **Use index cards to take notes on the text.**

- **The front of the index card will have important *direct notes* about the text.**

- **The back of the index card will have your *personal response* to the information.**

Direct Notes

On September 6, 1620 the Mayflower set sail for America with 102 Pilgrims aboard.

Personal Response

I think it must have been real scary for the Pilgrims taking a long trip to an unknown land.

Partner Interview

- **Interview your partner about a topic you are studying.**

- **As you ask questions, jot down important key words and short notes.**

- **When the interview is finished, use your notes to record the important information your partner said about each question.**

Person interviewed:

_____

Interview about:

_____

1. How did you learn about

_____?

2. What have you read about

_____?

3. What facts do you know about

_____?

4. Is there anything else you want to say about

_____?

Phone Book Conventions

- **Make a chart like this.**

- **Using a phone book with both white and yellow pages, notice the conventions and features in the book.**

- **In the boxes, write how each convention is important and helps the reader.**

Alphabetical Order	Guide Words
Index	**Bolded Words**
Headings	**Categorizing**

Picture This

● **Draw and write the key information about
_____ historical event from
the text.**

Picture:	Written Description:

Problem-Solution

- Make a chart like the one below.

- Complete the chart using the problem that was discussed in the text.

Problem in the Text:		
Why it Was Important:	**Steps Used to Solve the Problem:** 1. 2. 3. 4.	**How the Problem Was Finally Solved:**

Put Yourself in History

- **Look at the _____ event on page _____ of the text.**

- **Turn the event into a piece of historical fiction by rewriting the event with you included.**

Question Web

- **Think of a question you still have after reading the text.**

- **Write your question in the center of the web.**

- **Research the answer and complete the web.**

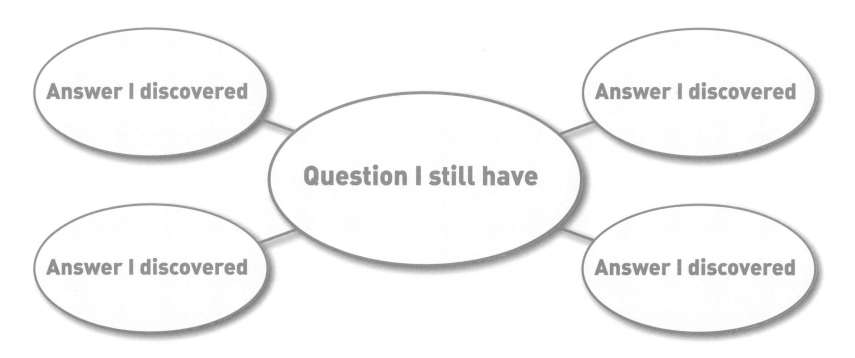

Research Follow-Up

- **Think of questions you still want to know after reading the text.**

- **Write them down on a chart like this one.**

- **Research the answers and fill in the chart.**

Questions I still have	Answers	Where I found the answers
1.		
2.		
3.		

Text Questions

- **Make a chart like the one below.**

- **Fill it out *before*, *during*, and *after* reading the text.**

- **After reading, if your questions were answered in the text, place a ✔ in each box.**

- **Research the questions that weren't answered and write the answers on the back of the chart.**

Before Reading Questions:
- ☐
- ☐
- ☐

During Reading Questions:
- ☐
- ☐
- ☐

After Reading Questions:
- ☐
- ☐
- ☐

This Is Your Life

- **Make a timeline depicting the life of _____ , who was discussed in the text.**

- **Be sure to include the most important information.**

- **Draw a picture of your famous person to go with your timeline.**

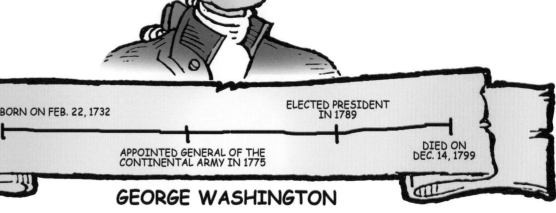

BORN ON FEB. 22, 1732

APPOINTED GENERAL OF THE CONTINENTAL ARMY IN 1775

ELECTED PRESIDENT IN 1789

DIED ON DEC. 14, 1799

GEORGE WASHINGTON

Timeline Sequencing Game

- **Write down the major events that happened in the text on index cards.**

- **Exchange the cards with your partner and see if he/she can arrange the cards in the correct order.**

- **Check yourself with the text.**

- **Take a sheet of paper and glue the cards in the correct order on it.**

- **Draw a picture to match each event.**

1728 – Opens his own printing office in Philadelphia

1752 – Performs the famous kite experiment

1706– Benjamin Franklin was born in Boston, Massachusetts

1776– Signs the Declaration of Independence

Two-Column Note-Taking

- **Fold a paper in half to take notes on the text.**

- **The left side will have the main idea of each paragraph or section of the text.**

- **The right side will have important details about the main idea.**

- **Use the main idea statements on the left-hand side to write a summary when finished.**

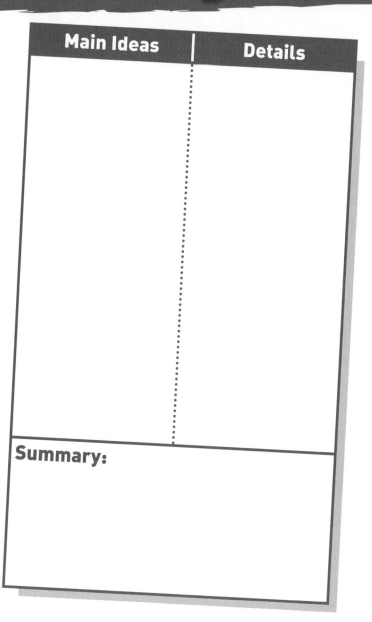

Main Ideas	Details

Summary:

Venn Diagram

- Copy the "modified" Venn diagram below.
- Use the information in the text to compare
  X: _____ and Y: _____

X: _____	Same about Both	Y: _____

What's New to You

- **Write down all the things you discovered from the text that you didn't know before.**

- **Write about what made each a new discovery for you.**

Word Cluster

- **Create a cluster based on the word** _____.

- **Use your text to help fill in the cluster.**

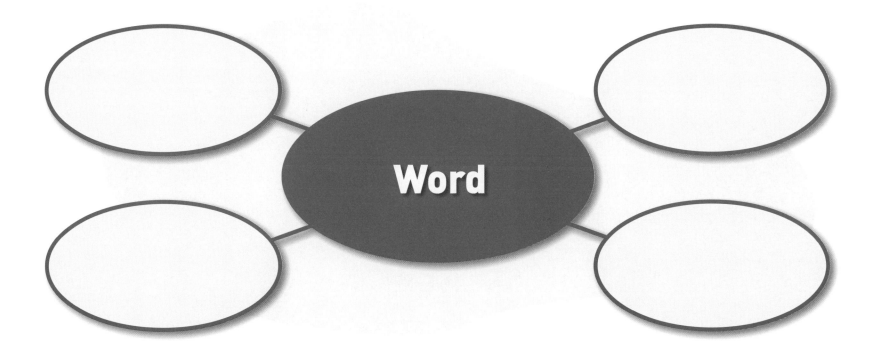

Word

References

Boyles, Nancy N. *Constructing Meaning Through Kid-Friendly Comprehension Strategy Instruction*. Gainesville, FL: Maupin House, 2004.

Burke, Jim. *Reading Reminders: Tools, Tips, and Techniques.* Portsmouth, NH: Boynton/Cook Publishers, Inc., 2000.

Calkins, Lucy McCormick. *The Art of Teaching Reading.* New York: Longman, 2001.

"Comprehension Instruction: Texas Reading Initiative." Texas Education Agency, 2000.

Fountas, Irene, Gay Su Pinnell. *Guided Reading: Good First Teaching for All Children.* Portsmouth, NH: Heinemann, 1996.

_____. *Guiding Readers & Writers (Grades 3-6): Teaching Comprehension, Genre, and Content Literacy.* Portsmouth, NH: Heinemann, 2000.

Goudvis, Anne, Stephanie Harvey. *Strategies That Work: Teaching Comprehension to Enhance Understanding.* York, ME: Stenhouse Publishers, 2000.

Harvey, Stephanie. *Nonfiction Matters: Reading, Writing, and Research in Grades 3-8.* Portland, ME: Stenhouse Publishers, 2000.

Keene, Ellen Oliver, Susan Zimmerman. *Mosaic of Thought: Teaching Comprehension in a Reader's Workshop.* Portsmouth, NH: Heinemann, 1997.

Miller, Debbie. *Reading with Meaning: Teaching Comprehension in the Primary Grades.* Portland, ME: Stenhouse Publishers, 2002.

"Promoting Vocabulary Development: Texas Reading Initiative," Texas Education Agency, 2000.

Stead, Tony. *Is That a Fact? Teaching Nonfiction Writing K-3.* Portland, ME: Stenhouse Publishers, 2002.

Stead, Tony. *Reality Checks: Teaching Reading Comprehension with Nonfiction K-5.* Portland, ME: Stenhouse Publishers, 2006.

Taberski, Sharon. *On Solid Ground: Strategies for Teaching Reading K-3.* Portsmouth, NH: Heinemann, 2000.

About the Author

Emily Cayuso is a campus instructional coordinator/reading specialist in San Antonio, Texas. She has taught a variety of primary grades and has worked as a reading recovery and Title 1 reading teacher specialist over the past thirty-three years. Emily has also served as a part-time adjunct faculty member at the University of Texas in San Antonio working with pre-service teachers. She conducts workshops for reading and language arts teachers. Recognized twice in "Who's Who Among America's Teachers," Emily is the author of *Designing Teaching Study Groups: A Guide for Success, Flip for Comprehension* and its Spanish translation, *Dar La Vuelta a la Comprensión*, and *Flip for Word Work*. She holds a B.S. and an M.Ed.